Crits

"This is a brilliant book. I love how you can personalise sections of the book for your own horse. We're new to this game and the book gives a step by step guide on everything you need to take care of your animal, from choosing stables to grooming and feed. You can tell that the author is passionate about her horses. All in all a really helpful book for somebody starting out." **Les Bone**

"A very informative book which is easy to follow and understand. The pictures and drawings are really helpful and ideal to add your own personal touch. Would definitely recommend to anybody seeking advice on the care of a horse or pony." **Joe Hayton**

My 1st Horse Book and Me

Tracy Scott

RoseTintedSpecs Imprint

Copyright Matters

ISBN 978-0-9927057-5-6 (paperback)
also available as an e-book ISBN 978-0-9927057-6-3 (.mobi/Kindle)

RoseTintedSpecs Imprint
Publisher: David G. Rose
Butchers Farm, Molash, Kent, United Kingdom
www.rosetintedspecs.com
e-mail: publisher@rosetintedspecs.com

Printed in the US and UK. British-English spelling is used in this book. Font licensing correct at time of publication

About Tracy the author

Do you know the saying "it's in your blood?" I can remember at the age of three sitting bareback behind my brother on our dad's horse. His dad and grandad (my great-grandfather pictured below) had also owned horses. Even though theirs were of the "working" type they still had the deep desire to own and care for them.

Our grandad told us stories of how in "those days" his horses had to work hard pulling bundles of kindling up and down the cobbled streets of Manchester where I was born. They didn't return home until the wagon was empty, sometimes in the wet and dark. Once back home he would always make sure the horse was fed and groomed and the stable comfortable before he went for his own tea.

The word "dedication" would pop up often and it is that word that remains in my mind.

At the age of five I began riding lessons at the local stables, an hour a week on my favourite pony Flicker. As I dismounted 'my' 12.2 hh Palomino pony and led her back to the yard I knew the next seven days would take forever to pass.

I continued with my lessons showing no sign of it being a fad and was lucky enough at the age of seven to be bought my first pony. My passion and devotion now really began.

When I left school I trained under Olympic instructors and became a qualified riding instructor. At 17 years old and with the help of my parents, I started my own riding centre. I was working on my dream becoming a reality. I started with just three ponies and one horse, worked seven days a week with very long hours and a lot of hard work, until after 15 years I had 16 horses and ponies.

I taught children and adults that riding was not only great fun but you could gain much more from a horse if you learnt more about him, his needs and how to look after him properly. This is a commitment that must be taken seriously. He is totally reliant on you for food, water and shelter but he will give you much back in return.

Tracy, pictured here with Kizzy, now lives and works in France. She is still involved with horses and rides regularly. She is very pleased to have written this book for you to read and enjoy.

Contents

YOUR SECTION IN THE BOOK!

My horse 41

If you are fortunate to have a horse or pony put pictures of him here and on page 42. Alternatively put in pictures of your favourite horse.

Description of my horse 43

Describe him here, his breed, height, age, colour and so on. Did the previous owner or vet tell you anything about him you need to watch out for? You could print any extra information and slip or glue the pages in.

Feeding my horse 44

Describe here what your horse likes and how you vary his feed according to the season and the work he does. This is particularly useful for the occasions you won't be able to feed him yourself.

Events and prizes 45

Describe here any cups, rosettes and other prizes you and your

Introduction

Most people can only dream of owning a horse. If you are fortunate enough to have one of your own you will know how much pleasure and fulfilment he can bring. For this, however, you have to be 110% committed to learning about horses in general and yours in particular.

Owning a horse or pony means you will be asking many questions and have problems to solve. There will be worrying times when he is sick or injured but the answers to your questions will come if you take the time to get to know and fully understand him and his ways.

Spending time with horses, watching their daily habits, how they socialise in the field with others, noting their "pecking" order and so on, is intriguing. Why does one chew a couple of mouthfuls of hay from one pile and move on to the next, pushing another horse away? Does he think that pile will be tastier or is he letting the other horse know who is boss? And why would he charge up and down the fence line when his companion is taken out of the field, only to greet him with his ears flat back and showing his hindquarters when he is returned?

One of the great joys of being involved with horses is riding them. Almost anyone from a young child to an elderly person can learn to ride. Your horse must be fit, healthy and amenable to this. Being able to recognise when a horse is ill or lame is a forever learning process. You feel a great sense of achievement when you have nursed a horse back to good health after an illness and feel more confident in yourself with the new knowledge and experience.

What you get from your horse depends on how much time and effort you put in to learning about him and his needs and how dedicated you are to grooming and exercising him. Don't expect his coat to gleam and shine, for example, if you only brush him once a week, or your tack to remain soft and supple if it is left on the floor

9

after a ride covered in sweat and dirt. Don't expect him to come to you when you call him in the field if you are not kind and patient with him.

If your ultimate aim is to become a horse master you must begin by learning how to recognise the normal, healthy behaviour and look of every horse you come into contact with. A good basic knowledge of horse care is your starting point. You will learn from your mistakes, you will learn something new every day and you might ultimately become an expert. On the way you will have the benefit and joy of owning a horse!

Choosing "which" riding stables

• is the establishment approved by the BHS (British Horse Society?)

• is your first impression "yes, this is how I imagined it!" rather than "oh no, let's get out of here ..."

• are the yard and stables clean and tidy?

• are the staff and helpers friendly and helpful?

• do the horses and ponies look healthy and happy?

• have they been brushed ready for riding?

• does the tack look clean and feel secure?

• are there correctly-fitting approved riding hats for hire?

You should also ask if your lessons will be given by a qualified instructor. Find out if the lessons are private or in a group. If in a group, ask how many. With more than six riders it can be a slow learning process. Ideally you should visit several stables until you find the right one for you.

A recommended riding stable is a good place to start and you will probably already have learned a lot from the person recommending it!

Enjoy your lessons!

Useful tips on buying a horse

The main point to establish is why you want a horse or pony and what you intend doing with him. A youngster's first pony must give him or her confidence. A young child and young pony are not a successful combination as neither know what is expected of him. A child's confidence is easily lost and rebuilding it can take weeks or months. Sometimes it is lost forever.

Think safety at all times when with horses.

1.   Always take an experienced horse person with you when going to look at a horse.

2.   Your first impression of the establishment will tell you a lot. Is it clean and tidy?

3.   Your first meeting with the horse will tell you plenty. Is he alert, with pricked ears and a large, generous, kind eye? These things indicate a good, gentle character.

4.   Watch how the horse reacts when being handled and having his tack put on.

5.   Ask for the horse to be walked and trotted in hand away from you and then towards you and past. Look how straight he moves and if he is sound and not limping.

6.   Check the horse all over. Stroke his head, pat his neck, run your hand down his legs past the flanks and over his quarters. Pick up each

---

British riding stable terminology

bombproof a horse that is reliable and safe and not likely to spook.

schoolmaster experienced horse in all activities and able to teach an inexperienced rider a lot.

green horse one that has been broken in and taught the basics.

aged a horse more than 15 years old.

foot in turn. Do not try these things if you have no experience with horses. Even if you have, you will not know the animal.

7.   If the horse already has his tack on ask to see him being tacked up. The owner may be trying to hide something.

8.   If the pony is for a child, make sure you see a child ride him. If he is used to being ridden by an adult he may be too strong for a young child.

Hands

A horse's height is measured in centimetres or hands. A hand is equal to four inches (10 cm.) The measurement is taken from the ground by the foreleg to the withers. The withers is the top of the shoulders, between neck and back.

A horse is classed as a horse when it is 14.2 hh (hands) or more, fully grown. The number 1, 2 or 3 after the decimal point indicates inches, so 14.3 hh is fourteen hands plus three inches.

9.   Let the seller ride the horse first so you can see how he is mounted. Does he stand still and relaxed? Ask that he be put through his paces walking, t r o t t i n g , cantering and galloping and to see him go over a jump if there is one. Ask the owner to ride out of the yard, down

Horse colours and patterns

appaloosa spotted.

bay red, yellow or brown with black mane and tail.

black all black except for some white markings.

brown black and brown mix.

buckskin light tan or brown.

chestnut yellowish tan.

dun sandy yellow or brown usually with darker legs, mane and tail.

grey black and white hair on black skin.

palomino golden yellow or cream all over with white mane and tail.

piebald with large black patches on white.

pinto and **paint** in the United States are general terms for horses with large patches of a darker colour on white.

roan can be red, blue (i.e. black or brown) or chestnut always mixed with white hair.

skewbald with large coloured patches (not black) on white.

white white hair on pink skin.

the road and back past the entrance to see he does not object to leaving his home.

10.   Look to see how he is managed from walk to trot, trot to canter, canter back to trot and so on. Does he remain calm?

11.   Does he stop easily and stand patiently?

12.   Ask to be shown his teeth and gums. Is he reluctant to have this done? The experienced horse person with you will know what to look for.

13.   A horse that does not lead quietly might also be difficult to get into a horse box or trailer.

14.   Now it is your turn to ride and assess the horse and whether you suit one another.

REMEMBER Owning a horse is a privilege. We take up riding because we choose to do so. The horse won't have a choice so always treat him with kindness. Buying your horse can be the easiest part. Commitment and observation are needed to ensure he is happy, healthy and safe at all times.

Preparing for your new horse's arrival

The moment you have been waiting for is almost here! Something that was just a dream is about to come true. Preparing for the arrival of a new horse or pony is really exciting. On the practical side it must be well thought out in advance.

You probably know where you pony has just come from. Having as much information as possible about him, the surroundings he is used to, his feeding and watering regime and other important details like this will determine how well he settles in with you.

Here is a check list you should already have answers for:

- is he used to companions or has he been living on his own?
- has he been living outside all the time or been stabled at night?
- if he has been stabled, what bedding is he used to?
- how many feeds is he used to, how much and what kind?
- is he allergic to anything?
- when was he last wormed?
- are his vaccinations up-to-date?
- is there anything about his character you should know about?

I remember being told AFTER buying a pony that he had no respect for electric fencing, in other words no fear of it. How true that was! Within ten minutes of his arrival he walked straight through ours without a second glance. He probably had been lucky and not yet received a shock, as the pulse is intermittent. The grass was definitely greener, as the saying goes, on the other side of the fence.

Before his arrival, walk around your field checking the fencing for loose posts or wire. Ensure the gate opens properly and can be securely latched. There is more on this subject on page 57. Look particularly for sharp objects such as broken glass or tin cans, general rubbish and holes in which he could damage his ankle. Check for poisonous plants, remembering to pull or dig them out with the roots intact. There is more about plants and trees and their fruit that is poisonous to horses in various degrees on page 61.

Clear the field of droppings. Check the water supply (there is more on this on pages 38 and 56), making sure it is fresh whether it is in a trough, buckets or from a stream. If he has a stable make sure the bedding is clean (see pages 66 to 69) with plenty of straw for comfort, water and hay in a manger or hay net.

REMEMBER He will be nervous, so allow a few days for him to settle in and get used to you and his surroundings. Everything, including smells, noises and the taste of the water will be different. Check on him regularly without fussing.

Your new adventures are about to begin!

Head markings

stripe/ strip narrow white mark running down the face.
blaze wider stripe down the face.
bald face a blaze with its width beyond the eyes.
white muzzle with white around the chin and lips up to the nostrils.
star mark on the forehead whether star-shaped or not.
snip white marking between the nostrils.

Markings can be further qualified as interrupted, irregular, connected and faint. These, along with leg and body markings are important in recognising individual horses, especially when there are a lot of them in the field.

Points of the horse

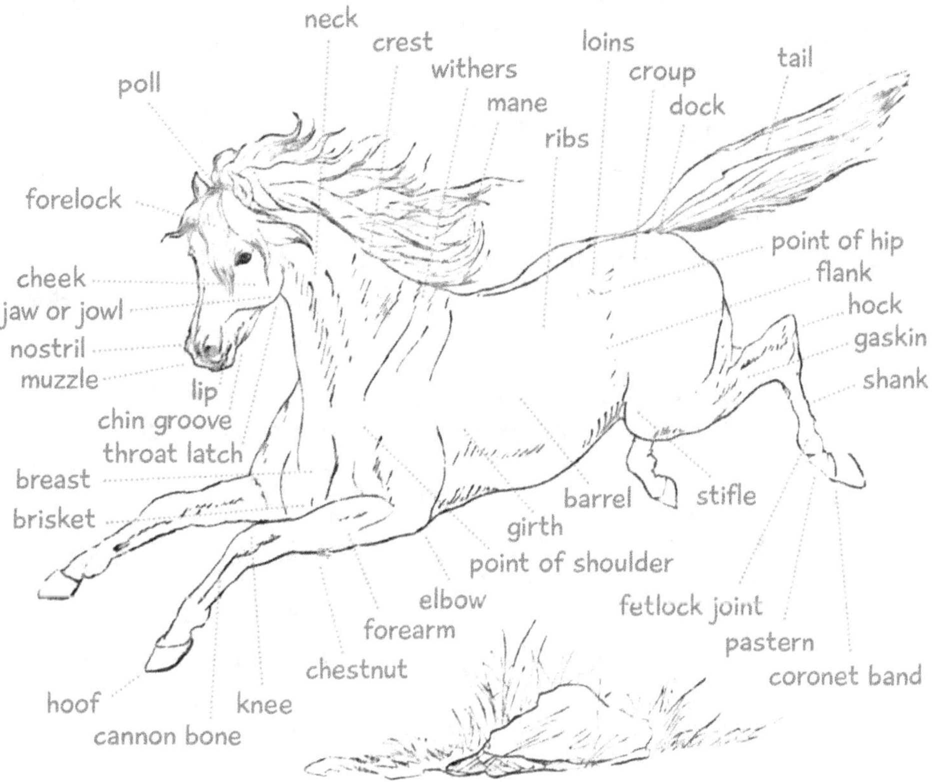

Points in more detail

The poll is the very top of the horse's skull. The crest is the upper
part of the neck where the mane grows. The withers is the bony
protrusion at the base of the neck where the mane ends and the
back begins. The croup runs from the top of the tail to the highest
part of the hindquarters. The barrel is the main body area. The girth
is the part of the barrel with the largest diameter around which the
saddle is fastened. The shank is the cannon bone on the hind leg.
The muzzle refers to the horse's chin, mouth and nostrils. Chestnuts
are the horny protrusions above the inside of the knees and below
the inside of the hocks.

Handling

The art of horse mastership is a continuous learning process. However long you have been handling horses you keep learning new things about them.

When dealing with horses there is a wrong way of doing things, of course. Sometimes there are several right ways. In general the correct way is the safe way for yourself and the horse. A horse is very much a creature of habit. He is more comfortable with the same thing being done at the same time each day. To be in sympathy with a horse and understanding his mentality is essential to success in looking after and owning horses.

Always be calm, speak quietly and handle gently but firmly, avoiding sudden movements. You must be confident while showing respect for the animal. These are the simplest and most important lessons to learn.

A word frequently repeated quickly becomes familiar to him. He learns also from the tone of your voice and manner in which the word, the command, is used. He will also

> ### Distinction between the domesticated and wild horse
>
> The horse (genus *Equus*) roamed Europe during the Pleistocene Period from about 2.5 million years ago to the start of the last Ice Age. Only three sub-species remain, the modern domesticated horse (*Equus ferus caballus*) and two wild sub-species, the Tarpan (*Equus ferus ferus*) and Przewalski Horse (*Equus ferus Przewalskii.*)
>
> The Tarpan, a small, dark brown untameable horse with black beard was extinct by the end of the 19th Century. The Przewalski Horse died out in the wild in the 1960s but there are several small herds around the world including in Wales and Denmark (see the picture on page 79). Many horses termed "wild," such as the Mustang in America and Brumby in Australia are actually descended from the domesticated horse.

recognise the voice of the one who feeds him or who is kind to him.

A good example of a command your horse should learn is "wait!" while you are opening or closing a gate or stall door, or putting his feed into a bucket. A horse with poor ground manners can be a danger to itself and to you. He should also be taught to stand quietly when tied, whether it is to have his hooves

cleaned or be groomed or tacked up, or simply so you can get on with other things.

When handling:

- always approach to the shoulder

- never rush. Take deliberate steps and speak as you advance

- when moving around him be quiet but confident

- when you are near enough, pat or stroke his neck or shoulder

- most horses do not like to be patted on the head on first contact and will raise their head or back away as in the picture above

- stroking the head with a downward movement will encourage him to relax. His head will lower when he feels more confident with you

- keep hand contact with him as you walk from the head, past the

neck, belly and flanks and around the hindquarters to the other side. This will let him know where you are at all times

• as your horse begins to recognise your voice he will, hopefully, come to you when called or know there will be a reward from you

• one reason a horse bites is because he is fed tit-bits such as sugar cubes and mints. Try not to feed these or spoil him generally. Reward him with an apple or carrot after he has behaved well

• horses that don't stand quietly when tied are often those that don't lead quietly either

TOP TIP Speak frequently to the horse and keep your body movements smooth.

It is a good idea to put a head collar on your horse and attach a lead rope when handling him. When you tie him up it should be done with a quick-release knot.

Firstly, make sure the horse is tied up in a safe and secure place where there is nothing for him to step on or knock over and where he is unable to move or pull something over. Gates, stable doors, garden furniture, motor vehicles, drainpipes and old fencing are **NOT** ideal. A tie-ring fixed into a wall at the horse's eye level is the safest.

Horses are flight animals. It is a natural instinct that enables them to get away from a predator. If startled, they are likely to pull back and if they feel a lead will give way they might pull even harder.

How to put on a head collar

1.   Undo the cheek piece.

2.   Approach the near side (the horse's left) and stand at the shoulder facing forwards.

3.   Slide the lead rope over the neck (to stop him moving away) then lift the noseband over the muzzle until it is halfway up the face and comfortable.

head collar

4.   Put your right hand under the throat and gently pass the cheek strap over the head behind the ears so it sits at the poll, then fasten it on the near side (left).

5.   Check it is straight and that you can fit two fingers behind the noseband and cheek piece.

> **TOP TIP** To clean a nylon head collar place it in a bucket of warm, soapy water and use an old toothbrush, especially on the noseband.

Always make sure the head collar is fitted correctly. They are made of leather or nylon and some have adjustable nosebands as well as cheek pieces.

How to tie a quick-release knot

1.   Always have a piece of string tied through the tie-ring and

knotted (as in the next diagram) before tying the lead rope through it. The horse can break free if in real danger.

2.	Put three-quarters of the lead rope through the string.

3.	Make a loop in the middle of the rope then make another loop to push through the first loop.

4.	Pull the rope above the loop back up towards the tie-ring.

5.	Put the end of the rope through the loop if your horse becomes wise to this knot and can undo it with his teeth.

6.	To untie, pull the free end of the lead rope (shown knotted here.)

> **TOP TIP** If the horse is reluctant to stand quietly when being tied up, attach a filled hay net to encourage him.

Leading a horse

A horse should be led with his shoulder level with the person leading him, with either a lead rope or reins attached to the bridle.

You should get a horse accustomed to being led from either side but when leading on a road you should be walking in the direction of the traffic (on the left in the UK) and on the horse's off side, that is, between the horse and the traffic.

When the horse is wearing a head collar, hold the rope with one hand just below the clip, keeping the free end of the rope in the other hand.

When leading in a bridle do not lead by holding the bit. Bring the reins over the horse's head and hold them with one hand a short distance from the bit. Hold the buckle end in the other hand.

To move the horse, speak to him and walk forward. Keep looking ahead. Most horses will refuse to move if stared in the face. If he holds back do not pull at his head. Push with your hand under the chin, repeat the command "walk on!" and move forward. If he still refuses to budge, tap his flank with a whip in your outside hand around your back, or get an assistant behind you to encourage him to move forward with a tap.

When turning, steady the horse and turn him from you by pushing his head away so you don't get your toes trodden on. Hold his head up with his hocks under him so he is balanced and under more control. When he does as he is asked, praise him with your voice and reward him with either a stroke or a pat. A stroke should be soothing. A pat is good for praising.

You should be positive and consistent in your orders and signals so your horse does not become confused. Decide what you are going to do, when you are going to do it and how you are going to do it so the horse clearly understands your message. Teaching your horse to lead properly is the basis of all good ground manners.

TOP TIP Wearing gloves can prevent rope burn if the horse suddenly pulls away.

Grooming

Grooming is necessary to keep your horse healthy and in good condition. It helps prevent disease caused by parasites that feed on dead hair and skin, ensures cleanliness and improves his appearance, something in which every proud owner is interested.

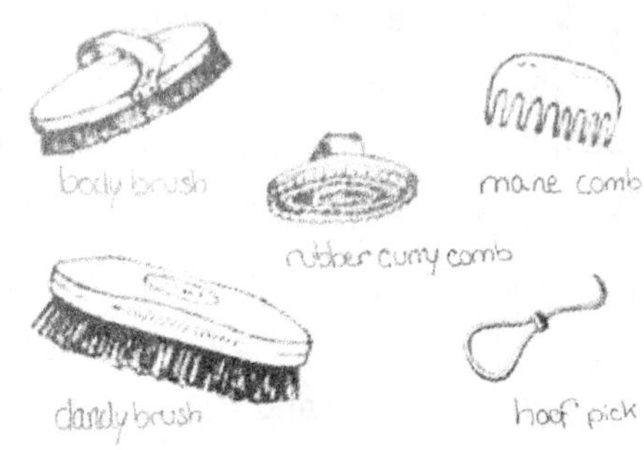

The stabled horse is unable to roll and exercise as he does in his natural environment. Because of this, skin and feet can suffer if proper care is not taken.

• daily grooming also helps to improve the relationship between horse and owner

• it relaxes the horse and enables the owner to inspect and observe him more closely

• removing sweat and keeping the pores open helps blood circulation and promotes good health

A typical grooming kit

1. Hoof pick (for cleaning the underside of the foot.)

2. Dandy brush (for removing caked mud and dirt.)

3. Body brush (to remove scurf - dead skin - and dust from the coat.)

4. Metal curry comb (for cleaning the body brush.)

5. Rubber curry comb (used on horses with heavy coats to help remove caked dirt and mud and when the horse is changing his coat.)

6. Sponges (one for cleaning eyes and nose and one for the dock area.)

7.   Tack tray to keep the grooming brushes in.

8.   Hoof oil and brush.

Before starting grooming put his head collar on and tie him up securely. Grooming is normally done in the following order:

Hoof pick

Always begin by picking out the feet. Start with the near forefoot and work around the horse, the same way each time. Begin by speaking to him and stroking his neck then turn to face the rear.

1.   Run your left hand down his leg, past the knee, onto the fetlock joint, gently squeeze and say "up!"

2.   If your horse is reluctant to lift his foot, he may be more inclined to do so if you lean against his shoulder and push his weight onto the other leg.

3.   Pick up the hoof and hold it in the palm of your left hand.

4.   Using the hoof pick in your right hand, work it in a downward movement from the heel to the toe, taking out mud and stones.

5.   Take care around and on top of the frog, the wedge-shaped tissue with groove running to

the centre of the underside of the hoof.

The general health of the feet can be inspected and if needed they can be washed. This should be done with an old dandy brush. Hold the foot over a bucket of cold water (rubber buckets without handles are best), dip the brush in the water and sweep over the foot in a downward direction, trying to avoid wetting the heels.

Rubber curry comb

Standing at the near side with the curry comb in the left hand, begin at the poll and work around the body in circular movements avoiding

the face and areas below the knees and hocks, as these are sensitive parts. Repeat the same process on the other side using the right hand.

Dandy brush

Starting at the poll, work with a flicking action, brushing out caked dirt or sweat marks. Pay special attention to the belly, knees, hocks, fetlocks, pasterns and to saddle marks. The dandy brush should not be used on sensitive parts and it should never be used with a heavy hand. Clean the dandy brush by brushing it over the curry comb.

Body brush

Starting on the left side at the poll, use long sweeping strokes all over the body following the direction of the hair. Work from the front of the horse to the back and from the top to the bottom so you do not brush dirt onto already clean parts. Repeat on the other side.

Holding the head collar with one hand, brush the face following the direction of the hair, taking care around the eyes and nose. Brush the mane to the opposite side to which it normally lies then brush it

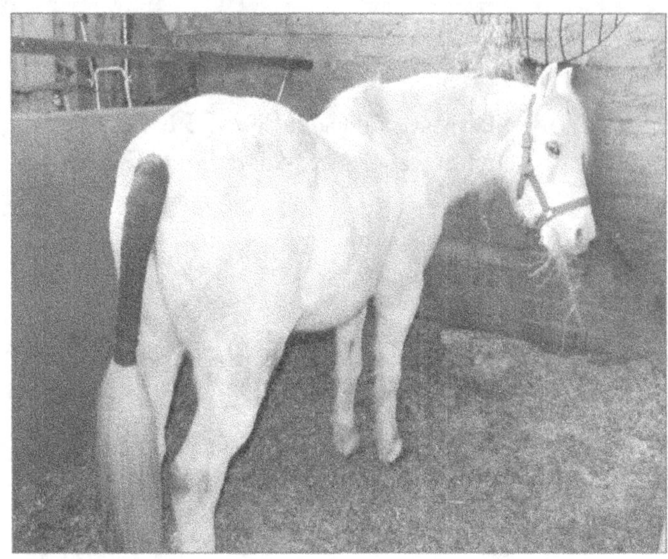

back again and lay it down flat.

After every four or five strokes of the body brush clean it with the metal curry comb.

> **TOP TIP** When washing brushes don't place them in very hot water as the bristles can shrink and become hard.

Metal curry comb

This is used to clean the body brushes, not the horse. Hold the handle of the comb and pass the body brush through it several times, sweeping it away from you. Bang the comb on your heel or toe to clean out the dirt rather than on a wall or floor as this can bend the metal.

Sponges (two)

Place the first sponge in a bucket of warm water and wring it out until it is soft and damp. Move to the horse's head and with one hand on the head collar gently clean out the corners and outer perimeters of the eyes. Rinse the sponge and wipe out the nostrils.

Next, move to the tail with the second sponge. Whilst talking to the horse and standing slightly to the side, lift up his tail and clean the whole dock region. Wash both sponges when finished. In the picture opposite, Fuggy's tail has been bandaged to keep it flat after grooming.

Hoof oil

Apply hoof oil to the underside and outside of the hooves to help prevent cracking and add a shine to the feet.

Thoroughness brings its own reward. A well-groomed horse is a pleasing sight, as in the picture below on a summer evening in the village of Leafield, Oxfordshire.

Health indications

A horse's coat is the mirror of his general health. The key to maintaining his health and fitness is to be able to spot differences in look and behaviour that are not normal. No one expects you to be an expert in the list of possible horse illnesses and ailments on the opposite page.

They are there for you to look up. Hopefully, you won't come across the terms except when your horse is vaccinated. You should, however, be the expert in how your horse is under normal circumstances.

For suggestions on what to keep in your medicine cabinet for you and your horse see the heading **First Aid** on page 33.

Signs of good health are:

- a glossy coat lying flat

- looking alert with ears pricking

- skin loose and supple and moving easily on the underlying bones

- membranes under the lids and the linings of the nostrils pink

- eyes open and bright

- the horse eating up well and chewing normally

- the body well filled out but not gross

- droppings vary in colour with the diet and should be passed approximately eight times daily in the form of balls, moist and free from offensive odour. When the horse is at grass, they may be looser but not as sloppy as a cow's

- limbs smooth and cool to the touch, not swollen or hot

- standing evenly on all four feet. Resting a hind leg but not a foreleg, is normal

- urine fairly thick and either colourless or pale yellow and passed several times a day

- a sound horse, taking strides of equal length with his weight spread evenly on all four legs

- breathing when at rest at a rate of 8 to 12 breaths per minute. This is most easily measured by watching the flanks. The nostrils and ribs should only move slightly

- temperature of 36 to 38 degrees Celsius (96.8 to 100.4 degrees Fahrenheit.) A rise of two or three degrees C often denotes pain. If it is more, the horse may have an infection

- pulse of 36 to 42 beats to the minute. A convenient place to take the heartbeat rate is on the inner surface of the under jaw

In general, a sick animal appears listless and is likely to be off his feed. His head may be lowered and his ears drooping. Gait and posture could be unsteady and he could be in poor condition.

If the horse is not thriving seek expert advice, having first satisfied yourself he is not overworked or under-fed and that his pulse, respiration and temperature are normal. Keep on worrying until you see an improvement! And don't be afraid to chat with the vet or farrier and ask general questions during routine vaccinations or shoeing.

Some common horse ailments

Botulism
Colic
Coughing disorders
EHV
EPM
Equine Anaemia
Equine Arthritis
Grass Sickness
Laminitis
Mange
melanoma
Rain Rot
Ringworm
Strangles
Sweet Itch
Tying-up syndrome

Vaccinations are routine against:

EPM
Equine Influenza
Rabies
Tetanus

So:

1.   Visit the horse every day and learn all you can about him.

2.   Note the indications of general good health.

3.   Feed him regularly according to the work he is doing.

4.   Give him a worming dose every eight weeks, or as recommended on the packet or by the vet.

5.   Have him inoculated against tetanus and influenza.

6.   Have his teeth checked regularly as they may be sharp and need rasping.

7.   Pick out his feet daily and check the condition of his shoes.

REMEMBER No foot, no horse.

 You should be aware of safety at all times. Accidents will happen and you must keep a First Aid kit in the stable or close by. This will help your confidence if a minor mishap, or even an emergency occurs. Make a note in a note book of any injury your pony sustains and how you dealt with it.

Store First Aid items in a clean dry box with a large red cross on it. It's a good idea to have the name and contact telephone number of your local vet and doctor on, or in the box as well.

Packaging must remain sterile, that is, unopened and not contaminated by air, water or dirt. Generally, once a bandage roll or anything in a sealed package has been opened and some of it used, the rest should be discarded. Remember to replace the item.

Here are my suggestions for items for your horse and for yourself and other people involved in looking after your horse.

1. Self-sticking bandages (two types.)

2. Surgical tape (for securing a bandage or swab.)

3. Antiseptic wound cleaner such as Betadine.

4. Cotton wool (for swabbing scratches and light cuts.)

5. Vaseline (for cracked heels.)

6. Zinc oxide cream (for minor skin irritation including sunburn.)

7. Wound spray or powder (for cuts and scrapes.)

8. Latex gloves.

9. Round-ended scissors.

10. Stable wraps/ standing wraps (for protecting legs from damage in a stall or when in pasture. They are also used to keep legs clean before a show.)

11. Gamgee or Animal Lintex (padding over a wound or poultice kept in place with a bandage or stable wrap.)

12.   Veterinary-type thermometer. Normal horse temperature is 36 C to 38 C. Use only if experienced.

13.   Clean plastic bowl.

14.   Wire cutters or bolt cutters (in case your horse becomes tangled in a wire fence.)

One of the most common injuries is having your foot stood on. It can be very painful and your foot and ankle can bruise very quickly. If this happens remove your footwear and sock and put your foot into a bucket of cold water or under a running tap as soon as possible. This will help stop or reduce swelling. Keep wiggling your toes. You may need to check that toe bones are not broken.

You must always wear strong shoes or boots because of this danger. Be aware a horse has two blind spots, immediately in front of him and immediately behind.

Getting to know your pony and his habits will help you recognise a situation in which he could injure himself, when he is off colour, or has an injury that needs attending to.

REMEMBER If in doubt about an injury to your horse, call your vet. If you are hurt, call the doctor.

Items for humans

antiseptic (such as Savlon or Dettol)

antiseptic cream (Savlon or Germolene)

bandages (crepe and cling type)

box of mixed plasters

wound cleaner (spray type)

cotton wool

gauze

round-ended scissors

surgical tape

Vaseline

Catching up and turning out

Catching up

Horses and ponies need catching frequently even if they are not going to be ridden. Some are not difficult to catch, others remain shy or wary. Many ponies make it difficult for an adult to catch them but are amenable to a younger person approaching.

Try to get a shy horse into the habit of coming to your call and associating your voice with a piece of bread or carrot. Never give sugar, it leads to nipping, jealousy, unwillingness to be caught and other bad habits. Giving treats is best done from a container so your fingers are not mistaken for carrots. Otherwise offer it on your palm with fingers together and bent well back.

Young or shy horses prefer to be gently rubbed on the shoulder or neck using your voice quietly, rather than being patted.

1. Firstly, slide a rope around the horse's neck. Take your time. Horses hate being hustled and can sense when you are in a hurry.

2. Put on the head collar, adjust if necessary, stroke his neck, take down the rope and hold it

correctly.

3.   Try not to let him assume every time he is caught he is to be ridden. This may lead to him becoming sour and refusing to be caught.

4.   Occasionally catching him, putting a head collar on, making a fuss of him and taking the head collar off again should intrigue him each time.

> **TOP TIP** If the horse is reluctant to be caught, catch his companion first.

Turning out

1.   Open the gate making sure it is wide enough for both of you to walk through without the horse catching his sides and also making sure it will not swing back on him.

2.   Walk through, then turn the horse around to face the gate as you close it.

3.   Pat the horse and walk a few steps away from the gate.

4.   Take off his head collar, pat him again and walk away.

5.   Turning a horse out in a head collar is not advisable as the horse may get caught when rubbing against

Horse extremes

The largest horse recorded in the UK was a Shire gelding named Mammoth. He stood 21.2 hh (2 m 18 cm) high and his peak weight was estimated at 3,300 lbs (1,500 kg.)

The largest breed is the Shire, the heaviest, the Brabant. By contrast Falabella miniature horses rarely grow to more than eight hands (81 cm.)

a tree or when leaning over the fence. He could even get the heel of his shoe caught in the collar when scratching his head or ears with a hind foot.

TOP TIP Offering him a piece of carrot before you take off his head collar will encourage him to stand at your side, even when the head collar is off.

Never hustle a horse by waving the head collar at him to make him gallop off. This can make him excitable and anxious when he is turned out in the future. Most horses soon learn the same simple drill if care is taken each time. A horse that is difficult to catch is usually the result of him not being turned out correctly.

The New Forest Ponies pictured below on the main road into Beaulieu, Hampshire will be blissfully unaware of this problem.

Watering

The importance of a clean, fresh supply of water cannot be too strongly emphasised. Nothing can affect the condition of a horse as quickly as insufficient water and water that is not clean. An indication that a horse is dehydrated is when his flanks are sunken.

• a horse drinks between six and ten gallons (27 and 45 litres) of water a day. Fifty per cent of the adult horse's body consists of water. Without water, blood circulation is impaired and digestion becomes impossible

• water is necessary to keep his temperature down

• if water is not constantly available, offer a drink before feeding. For the horse to get the full benefit of his food, leave one hour after feeding before offering water again

• if a bucket of water is left with the horse, change it by emptying, swilling out and refilling. Do this twice a day. Standing water soon becomes flat and stagnant

• horses that have been deprived of water should not be given as much as they can drink. It should be given in small quantities frequently until their system is back to normal

• keep troughs, buckets and drinkers clean and free of leaves and mud to avoid a build-up of slime

Knowing that water is available, a horse will drink when necessary. An outside trough with ice on it will not harm the horse but always crack and remove the ice. Some horses can break it with their foot. They can't do it with their mouth.

A horse that is hot and sweating seldom comes to harm if he takes a full drink of cool water and is walked around afterwards.

Watering in a stable

The most satisfactory way of providing water is to use buckets or an automatic drinking bowl. There are more reminders of the importance of watering on pages 56 and 65.

Watering at grass

When a horse is kept at grass a stream running by the field can be very useful especially if there is a good approach and the water is running over gravel. A shallow stream with a sandy bottom may result in the horse taking up a small quantity of sand when he drinks. This can cause sand colic. In times of drought, pollutants will be more concentrated in a natural water supply. The appearance of algae will also tell you something suspicious is going on upstream or around the pond. Horses are very sensitive to tastes and smells so he may already have alerted you.

There are more watering tips under the heading **The grass-kept pony** on page 55.

REMEMBER A horse will die without water.

Ponds

If the water supply in the field is a pond of stagnant water an alternative supply must be arranged.

Troughs

An automatic trough that re-fills is the best arrangement for watering horses kept at grass. Iron troughs are excellent. They must have an outlet at the bottom for emptying. They should be away from trees so leaves do not collect in them.

The ball cock should be in an enclosed compartment at one end. The trough is topped-up automatically as the horse drinks and wind and hot sun evaporate it.

Troughs require regular inspection, emptying and cleaning. During very cold periods, snow and ice must be removed. If there is no water supply in the field it has to be brought in every day by hand. Whatever type of container is used it must be placed firmly on the ground so the horse cannot knock it over or the wind blow it away, particularly when it is half empty.

TOP TIP Placing a football in a water trough when cold weather is expected will help keep it ice-free.

My horse

Description of my horse

Name :   Breed :

Year of birth :   Height :

Weight :   Date acquired :

Colour :

Body markings :

Face and leg markings :

Approximate worming dates :

Vaccinations :

NOTES :

Feeding my horse

No. of feeds per day in Summer :   in Winter :

Describe his summer feed regime :

Describe his winter feed regime :

Treats he likes :

Supplements :

Medicines :

NOTES :

Events and prizes

List the events in which you entered your horse giving the DATE, EVENT NAME, PLACE and PRIZES WON

Professionals to contact

Veterinarian :
Assistant/ secretary :
Address :

Telephone :   Mobile :
Web site :
NOTES :

Farrier :
Assistant/ secretary :
Address :

Telephone :   Mobile :
Web site :
NOTES :

Doctor :
Secretary/ receptionist :
Address :

Telephone :   Mobile :
Health Centre/ hospital :
Telephone :
NOTES :

Best places to buy feed and tack

Shop or outlet name :

Address :

Telephone :

Web site :

NOTE :

Shop or outlet name :

Address :

Telephone :

Web site :

NOTE :

Accident Report

Put the DATE of any accidents when you or your horse needed attention and note how you dealt with it.

A thoroughbred racehorse on its way back to the paddock after a race.

Horses to bring to life!

A Bay Hunter by the famous painter of horses, George Stubs, 1782.

Leonardo da Vinci
was commissioned in
1482 to make the
largest bronze horse
in the world standing
24 feet high. A rider
in armour would have
raised it to 36 feet.

The boy touching
the front hoof
shows its scale.

Preparing for shows and competitions

For many of us the most exciting part of taking part in a show is the preparation. There is nothing more satisfying than you and your horse

being well turned out and getting compliments from family and strangers alike. Grooming normally starts the day before the event.

If the weather is good and warm, begin with tying the pony to his usual tie-ring and brush him down. After picking out his feet wash the inside and outside of his hooves with an old dandy brush or toothbrush. Next, prepare a couple of buckets of warm water and have a large sponge, soft brush and horse shampoo handy. Don't use your normal hair shampoo as your horse's skin can be more sensitive than yours.

Start by washing his tail. If it is your first time, or the pony is nervous and keeps moving around you will need a helper. This part of the grooming is usually easier with two.

Continue talking calmly while you lift up the bucket with the sponge in it and slowly submerge his tail up to the dock. Then, holding the bucket close to the pony with one hand, use the other hand (or ask your helper) to sponge the very top of the tail. Put the bucket to one side on the floor, put shampoo on his tail and rub thoroughly into the roots. You will be surprised how much dirt you wash out!

Rinse by putting his tail into the bucket again and repeat until the water runs clear. Then, standing to one side hold the end of his tail and spin it around and around to remove the water. Be warned, you will get very wet doing this!

Next, start at the bottom of each of his legs working your way up with the sponge dipped into the warm water. If this unsettles him squeeze out the sponge so the water isn't running down his legs. Once the legs are damp continue up the neck and wash the mane thoroughly. Continue along his back and sides adding shampoo a little at a time to make a good lather. Rinse him thoroughly with clean water. Make sure you rinse all the shampoo out and the water is running clear.

When you have finished this, use a sweat scraper to remove as much water as possible from his coat so he doesn't catch cold. It

might take a while for him to get used to having a 'bath.' Some never really accept it but you must persevere.

Walk him around for ten minutes then tie him up again with a hay net to encourage him to stand still for the next stage, brushing his mane and tail.

Brush out mane and tail to get rid of knots and make everything look neat. If you would like his tail to look 'full,' divide it from the dock downwards and make a simple plait. Finish off by putting a bandage on it to keep it clean.

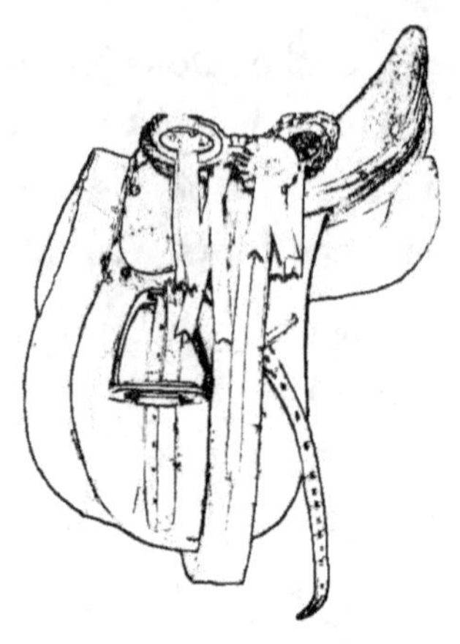

You can also plait part or all of his mane if you have time and the expertise, as in the picture left. Don't forget to clean and polish all metal bits as well as the leather on the bridle and saddle.

If the pony is in the stable for the night ensure it is clean and he has a rug to keep him warm and clean after his bath.

Enjoy the show and good luck in winning rosettes!

The grass-kept pony

Horses are happy and contented at grass and will be at their best when their few needs are attended to regularly.

They thrive in a properly-managed natural system and there are considerable savings in labour and costs. The picture right shows Comtois horses in Aveyron, South-West France in rich pasture.

A grass-kept horse exercises himself sufficiently. He is also able to roll in natural conditions whenever he feels inclined, sometimes after a good grooming when he was looking great! The picture on the next page shows a foal rolling in Charente-Maritime in Central France under the watchful eye of its mother.

Why do horses roll? In springtime it helps the removal of their winter coat. They also do it after work to ease the spots that have been subjected to pressure. As it gets colder, a layer of mud helps keep out the cold and wind and retain warmth. It is obvious that rolling is also an act of sheer enjoyment and should be encouraged!

The keeping of a horse at grass requires careful use of land that includes temporary fencing off if there is too much for the number of animals. Horses do not know when they have eaten enough and will eat all day long if given the chance. They are also a wasteful grazing animal. In their search for the most palatable grasses they will trample on valuable food.

How much land is needed to support a horse depends on the terrain, drainage and quality of grass. If he is at grass throughout the year, one-and-a-half to two acres (0,8 hectares) is a good guide.

Grass begins growing in April. It is at its best from mid-May until early July. By October the goodness has mostly gone and it will have stopped growing, though seasons are changing everywhere. From mid-September hay should be the horse's main bulk food. Put down an extra pile to the number of horses so those at the lower end of the "pecking order" get a fair share.

Water

The field must have water available at all times. If there is no supply it must be brought in daily by hand. There are pros and cons for the different types of supply but the best is a stream that does not dry up. Automatic water troughs should be cleaned out weekly. In winter, watch out for ice and the possibility of frozen pipes. Ice must be removed from a trough. Your horse will drink less over the winter but if he is not drinking enough, offer him warm water.

Avoid leaving buckets with handles in the field. If they are spilled or emptied a horse can get his foot caught in the handle. Put the bucket inside an old tyre where it is more protected from the wind. This will stop it from blowing around the field.

Gates

- gates should open fully, close firmly and have a secure latch

- a horse will become anxious if he catches his flank every time he is led through a narrow opening

- gates tied with string or looped around with wire are not secure. Your horse could more easily stray on to a road

- the ideal gate should be of a height your horse cannot jump

- five-bar metal gates are good and strong. They are also about five feet high and gate and latch are not chewable

Fencing

Fencing needed for horses is different from that of other stock. Horses readily get injured on ordinary fencing, especially when they try jumping it.

The cost of erecting and maintaining posts and rails is high but they are the first choice, as those in these two pictures of a Welsh Fell Pony near Llanymynech, Powys. Fencing should be put up inside an existing hedge boundary. Hedging alone is not good enough as the horse will find weak

spots. He will nibble at them and could make a gap through which he can escape.

Post and straight wire fencing is a cheaper, acceptable alternative. The wire must always be taut and the posts firm. All fencing should be kept in good repair. Old wire fences, particularly those with barbed wire, can be very dangerous. Horses attempting to jump these can be left with scars and torn tissue on their legs and chest.

Quite often a horse will paw at a stock fence and get his foot trapped, leading him to panic and pull until the fence gives or he gets a bad cut or injury.

Electric fencing has the advantage of being easy to put up and take down for when you need it somewhere else. If it is put up away from mains electricity you will need to check the charge level of the battery box and that the tape is not broken or touching leaves or branches. It is an effective way of keeping horses in a field because they quickly learn to respect the shock the charge can give.

REMEMBER Inspect fences while on your daily walk.

Shelter

Shelter from rain and wind is essential in Winter and from sun and flies in Summer.

- it can be a building, shed, high hedge or shady trees

- some horses use their sheds only when flies are pestering them

- cobwebs in sheds and stables are useful because they trap flies but ask if there is a potential fire risk

- ideally the shelter should be in a corner with the back to the prevailing wind

Healthy on the inside

A big problem with grass-kept horses is intestinal worms. If not dealt with they can cause internal damage. A horse's poor condition could be due to worm infestation. The worms live in the lining of the bowel and affect the digestion. This can cause diarrhoea, loss of weight, a staring coat and colic. They can even cause death if the owner does not realise how heavily infected the animal is.

Their prevalence is greatest in fields that are over-grazed or even continuously grazed, especially if the droppings are not collected up.

This should be done weekly, or if not practicable it should be spread around with a rake. Worming drugs are constantly being developed to make them more lethal to the parasite and less harmful to your horse. Seek advice on worming medicines before choosing. It's a good idea to change the brand periodically so the worms do not build up immunity to a particular one.

The following points will help prevent worm infection:

•	collect the droppings from your field weekly

•	chain-harrow or rake your field to break up manure piles and expose worm eggs and larvae to the elements

•	don't overgraze your field. If possible rotate with sheep or cattle to help interrupt the life-cycle of the parasite

•	alternate de-worming drugs so the parasite does not build up resistance to them

•	ask your vet what is an effective de-worming programme

•	good de-worming goes a long way to maximizing your horse's appearance, performance and comfort. Make sure he is as healthy on the inside as he is on the outside!

Poisonous plants

Look out for plants and trees in and around the field that are poisonous to horses. These must be removed and leaves and seeds from the trees, including acorns and conkers cleared away. There are dozens that are poisonous to varying degrees and it is worth looking them up and learning to recognise them. If you think your horse has eaten something toxic you must call the vet.

Of the list below, Ragwort and Yew in particular need to be burnt away from the field. Fresh, dead or dying, they are deadly poisonous to horses.

Some plants and trees poisonous to horses

Azalea	Foxglove	Plum trees
Boxwood	Ground Ivy	Poppy
Bracken fern	Hemlock	Potato
Broom	Horse Chestnut tree	Privet
Buckthorn	(and conkers)	Ragwort
Buttercup	Horse Radish	Rhubarb
Celandine, Greater	Iris	Rhododendron
Cherry trees	Laburnum	Walnut tree
Chickweed	Lily of the Valley	Woody Nightshade
Clover	Lupin	Yew
Cuckoo Pint	Marsh Marigold	
Deadly Nightshade	Oak tree (and acorns)	

One or more animals in a field

It is kinder to turn out two horses, or one horse and a donkey companion. A horse on his own can feel insecure and have a miserable time with flies during the Summer. You will often see horses in tight groups or in line using their tails as fly swatters for the benefit of those behind. They also huddle together to protect each other from rain and wind.

To sum up the needs of a horse or pony kept out at grass:
- catch him every day and check him all over, including his feet

- check around the field regularly picking up droppings, looking for holes that could damage his ankles, seeing that gates and fences are secure and picking up litter and glass if you are near a road

- fresh clean water always

- change grazing

- give hay as grass declines

- provide shelter from heat, flies and wet, windy weather

- ideally have another horse for companionship

REMEMBER Horses out of sight need as much attention as stabled horses you can see from your house.

The stabled horse

The main points about stabling are:

- construction and drainage
- the size of the stable relative to the size of the horse
- ventilation
- fittings (lights, switches, pipes, tie-rings, mangers etc.)
- bedding
- watering

The construction

Stabling is convenient to the owner. The horse is at hand, is clean and dry in bad weather and is easier to feed and water. It provides security and safety and is essential in cases of sickness when isolation is needed. The building should be sited with the back to the prevailing wind. It must be strong and made preferably of concrete blocks, stone or brick. Lining the inside with sheet material (like

chipboard, insulation board or plywood) or wooden boarding helps keep damp out and heat in.

Ideally, the roof should overhang at the front by three to four feet (a metre) for extra shelter and shade. A tile or slate roof is more durable than sheet metal. There should be a layer of roofing felt and an insulating sheet material on the underside.

The floor should slope slightly towards the door for drainage. Concrete with a roughened surface is the most common floor material. Feed mangers and hay nets should be sited away from drains. The main drainage outlet point should be at the front of the building away from the door.

> **TOP TIP** If tools are stored hung on a wall turn the prongs towards the wall to avoid you or your horse walking into them.

Dimensions

- the stable should be big enough for the horse to be led in and turned around

- a guide is 14 feet x 12 feet (3,5 metres x 4,5 metres) for a horse and 10 ft x 12 ft (3 m x 3,5 m) for a pony

- the door should open outwards, be at least 4 ft (1,20 m) wide and high enough for the horse to walk in and out without having to lower his head

- the door should be in two sections with the lower part fitted with two bolts, the bottom one being foot operated (a kick bolt)

- keep the top section open and latched to the outside wall. Horses greatly appreciate being able to see what is going on around them!

Ventilation

- horses are less likely to get coughs and colds with fresh air in the stable all year

- put another rug on the horse rather than close the upper half of the door during Winter

- the window should be on the same side as the door so there is no through-draught

- the window should be top-hinged so there is no draught on the horse's back

- use wired window glass or have a protective grill so the horse cannot injure himself on broken glass

Watering

As with grass-kept horses, fresh water must be available at all times. If you're using buckets, attach them to spring clips in corners so they don't get knocked over. Automatic water bowls are the most efficient but do not place them near a feed manger or hay rack as they soon become clogged with food.

Change the water twice a day and clean out the containers daily.

Fittings

Electric light fittings should be out of reach of the inquisitive horse's mouth and protected with wire mesh. All switches must be of a type designed for stables and fitted on

the outside. A horse could be electrocuted if he got his teeth around one. There should be no cable or piping at a height the horse could sever with his hooves.

A secure tie-ring at head height for tying up the horse whilst mucking out and grooming is essential. Tie a piece of strong cord to the ring and tie the lead rope to the cord (see page 22). It will secure him but give way should he have good reason to free himself.

Feeding mangers should be at the horse's chest height and preferably in a corner. Removable plastic mangers are more easily cleaned. Remove bucket handles so the horse can't get his foot caught in them.

Bedding

Bedding provides comfort and insulation against damp, cold and draughts. It protects a horse from injury and helps prevent him getting cast. This happens when he lays down or rolls so close to a fence or wall he can't stretch his legs and get up again without help. Should this happen you will need experienced help to get him on his feet again. Cast is more common in the confines of a stall.

Straw is the best bedding material because it is warm and comfortable when banked up around the walls and doors. It is readily obtainable and easy to store.

Wheat straw is recommended because it is easy to handle, warm, bright in appearance and has good free drainage. Barley is usually cheaper but is rougher and can irritate the skin. Oat straw makes good bedding but is more palatable and horses tend to eat it. It is also more porous and can quickly become soggy.

Never use damp or musty straw of any kind. Find a local farmer so you can see and smell the straw and hay before buying. If it is mouldy or dusty it can give your horse a very bad cough.

Wood shavings/ sawdust/ shredded paper can be used individually or mixed and is inedible. It makes a good, clean, bright and comfortable bed and is usually economical. The disadvantage of these materials is that there is no free drainage, it is not as easily handled as straw and more time is needed in the care of the bed.

Rubber matting creates a warmer, softer flooring than concrete or earth and makes cleaning and disinfecting of the bedding area quicker and easier. However, horses don't like lying on bare mats and you will still have to put some traditional straw bedding down for comfort. Rubber matting is dust free, drains well and saves on bedding costs in the long term.

Mucking out

For mucking out a stable you will need gloves, a pitchfork, shovel, hard sweeping brush, rake, skip and wheelbarrow. For washing a concrete floor that is clear of bedding you will need a hosepipe connected to a tap, or buckets of water and disinfectant. A high-pressure hose can be very useful.

Remove droppings regularly throughout the day. Muck the stable out and replenish the bedding daily. Clean stabling is the mark of a true horseman.

Renewing a straw bed

1.   Gather the tools outside the stable.

2.   Tie up the horse to the tie-ring. Place the wheelbarrow just outside the entrance to the stable.

3.   Start by clearing one corner separating any clean straw from the soiled straw with the pitchfork.

4.   Put the clean straw to one side and the dirty and wet stuff into the wheelbarrow.

5.   Work your way around the bedding using your pitchfork away from the horse, moving him to one side when needed.

6.   Sweep out the floor and leave to dry for a short while.

7.   When bedding down, put the clean used straw down first with the new straw on top. Baled straw should be well tossed. Push up more bedding around the sides of the stall.

8.   Sweep the doorway clean, remove and wash out the feed manger and re-fill the water buckets.

9.   Close the door on the inside, untie the horse and remove his head collar.

Renewing a sawdust bed

1.   Again, gather the tools you will need and put them outside the stable.

2.   Tie up the horse.

3.   Remove the droppings by hand or with a small rake and put them in a skip, laundry basket or plastic crate with grills as in the picture opposite. Remove the wet patches with a shovel.

4.   Rake the dry shavings from the sides of the stable into the centre so the bedding is even. Do not dig deep.

5.   Skip out frequently. Droppings break up easily and make mucking out more time-consuming.

REMEMBER Cleanliness is vital. Germs, disease and infection thrive in dirty conditions.

Feeding

Good, regular feeding is essential for a healthy, contented horse.

- it keeps him alive

- keeps him warm

- keeps him in good condition

- gives him the energy to do the work required

You must always be aware of your horse's needs and whether he has enough of the right type of food. Horses have a small stomach for their size and eat little and often. This means they have energy at all times and will not be bloated and inactive while a big meal digests.

That's not a problem for the scrap metal sculpture pictured right by *forgeron* (blacksmith) André Debru in Aveyron, South-West France!

Grazing is natural to a horse. When he is in work or stabled you will need to supplement or even substitute this natural regime with dry concentrates, hay and other things.

Much of a horse's food goes into keeping him warm.

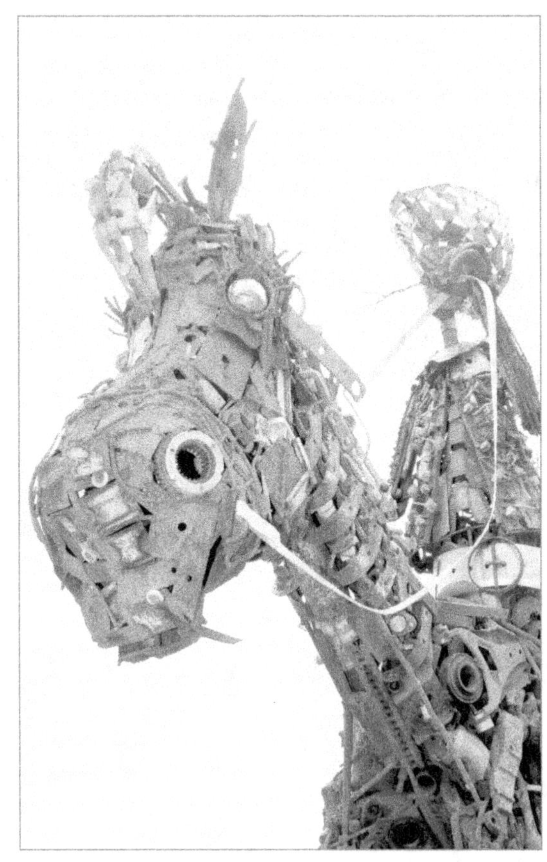

While fresh air is essential, reducing the loss of body heat means he will require less food for warmth. Draught-free stabling or a shelter outside and sensible use of rugs is essential.

Types of feed

The amount you feed your horse depends on his size, age and temperament, the type of work he is doing and whether he is stabled or at grass. The amount also varies with the season. Horses are individuals and feeding will vary from day to day. An experienced horse person sees how horses behave after feeding and is able to adjust their feed accordingly. This level of expertise takes time and shows a real love of horses.

A simple way of determining how much food a horse needs each day is to double his height and turn it into pounds, as in the chart on the next page. It is on the generous side so take off a couple of pounds for a horse and a couple more for a pony depending on whether he is a good doer (makes good use of his food) or a poor doer (has difficulty in keeping weight on). Putting on too much body fat can be a problem at any time.

REMEMBER The figures are for a horse and pony that are stabled and ridden every day.

Hay

Give plenty of good quality sweet-smelling hay. Avoid hay that contains docks, thistles and other plants. It is best not to feed hay that is less than six months old as it can cause digestive upsets. Store it on wooden slats. This allows air to circulate underneath it and prevent damp from rising into the bales.

How to calculate your horse's daily food needs

A 16 hh horse doubled = 32 lbs (14,5 kg). Take off two pounds = 30 lbs (13,6 kg) of food per day.

That is: 20 lbs (9,0 kg) of hay + 10 lbs (4,5 kg) of concentrates.

A 13 hh pony doubled = 26 lbs (11,8 kg). Take off 7 lbs (3,2 kg) = 19 lbs (8,6 kg) of food per day.

That is: 15 lbs (6,8 kg) of hay + 4 lbs (1,8 kg) of concentrates.

Chaff or chop

This is hay that has been passed through a 'chaff cutter' and mixed with the concentrated food. It adds bulk to an oat feed, ensures better chewing and saliva production and is good at stopping a horse from bolting (rushing) his food.

Horsage

A mixture of hay and silage, horsage is particularly useful for horses that are allergic to hay or straw. Care should be taken when feeding the high protein variety.

Concentrates

Horse/ pony cubes

These are manufactured and contain many ingredients including vitamins. They are clean to handle, easy to feed and are consistent in quality. They include oats, bran, maize, barley, linseed cake, nut meal, grass meal and molasses and are shaped like nuts or cubes. They are ideal for horses and ponies of first-time owners.

Cubes are quite expensive and your horse could find the same food every day monotonous. Be kind to him and add fresh carrots, apples and bread. Always check the sell-by date of compound feeds as they deteriorate when stored for long periods. Make sure you know which cubes you are feeding as they look similar.

Oats

Oats are the best all-round food for horses but must be fed sparingly to excitable ponies. Ponies that 'hot up' are difficult to handle and ride. The cereal can be fed bruised, crushed or rolled. It should not be stored for more than about three weeks because it goes stale. Oats are best fed mixed with chaff.

Sugar beet pulp

Dried sugar beet pulp must always be soaked in cold water for 24 hours before being fed to a horse. If it is fed dry it will cause choking or may swell in the horse's stomach and cause colic. It helps maintain a horse's weight and provides heat and bulk for a horse that only does a little work. It is also a source of energy and roughage. When preparing, mix 2.5 parts water to 1 part pulp.

Bran mash

This is a very useful warm food after hard exercise or for a horse that is run-down or has a slight cold. It is also a convenient way to administer medicines such as a cough remedy or worming compound.

To make a bran mash, half fill a bucket with bran, pour boiling water over it but do not saturate, stir in a spoonful of salt, add a handful of oats or barley, cover the bucket with a sack and leave to cool. A bran mash has a laxative value and is recommended for older horses once a week.

Barley and maize (flaked)

Rolled, crushed or preferably flaked, these two cereals can be fed on their own instead of oats. They have a similar food value but are not as likely to cause the horse to 'hot up.' Maize should be fed sparingly.

Boiled barley is a good pick-me-up for tired or sick horses and will often tempt a delicate feeder. To prepare, bring the barley to the boil and leave to simmer until the grains split. This takes four to six hours. Both barley and maize add variety to the diet and are good for putting fat on a horse. In the picture below, the horses, full of energy, are enjoying a work-out on the water's edge at Perranporth in Devon on a winter morning.

Linseed

This encourages a glossy coat and helps to condition the horse. It can be fed as a 'jelly' or 'tea' and is excellent for horses and ponies living out in the winter.

To prepare, put a handful into a saucepan, cover with water and soak overnight. The next day, add more water and bring to the boil. Remember, linseed that has not been boiled is dangerous. When cool it should set like a jelly that can be mixed with the evening feed.

Coarse mix

This is another manufactured product with the different feeds mixed together with chopped hay and molasses that gives it a slightly sticky feel. The grains are distinct and the mix ensures a well-balanced diet.

Rules of good feeding

- feed little and often. Try to imitate a horse's natural regime

- feed plenty of roughage (hay)

- feed according to the work the horse is doing and to his size, age and temperament

- make no sudden changes in diet or routine. Make any adjustments over several days

- feed at the same time each day. Horses like routine

- keep food buckets and mangers scrupulously clean

- throw away feed left over from the previous day

- feed only good, clean, quality forage

- offer water before feeding. His feed will not then be washed through his stomach

- do not work a horse immediately after a full feed or when his stomach is full of grass. Allow at least an hour for it to be digested

- give him something succulent every day if possible such as green foodstuffs, apples or carrots. This compensates for lack of grass

Store all feedstuffs in bins rather than in feed bags or their original sacks. This will discourage vermin. Weigh each horse's food. Keep a separate scoop for each food and keep them clean.

> **TOP TIP** Keep a feeding chart in the 'feed room' with the amount and type of food for each horse (see the picture on page 74.) This is really necessary where there are a lot of horses.

When NOT to feed

- if the horse is weak from a long fasting or is in very poor condition.

Be particularly careful to feed only small quantities at frequent intervals

• if the horse is very hot after work. His stomach cannot digest food properly

• if the horse is exhausted after exercise. Allow him to rest for an hour or two first

REMEMBER Horses are individuals and you should adjust the feeding regime to each animal.

Looking after a horse is a real commitment. He is totally reliant on you for all his daily needs. Look after him well, show patience and kindness and always remember the three letters **TLC**, Tender Loving Care!

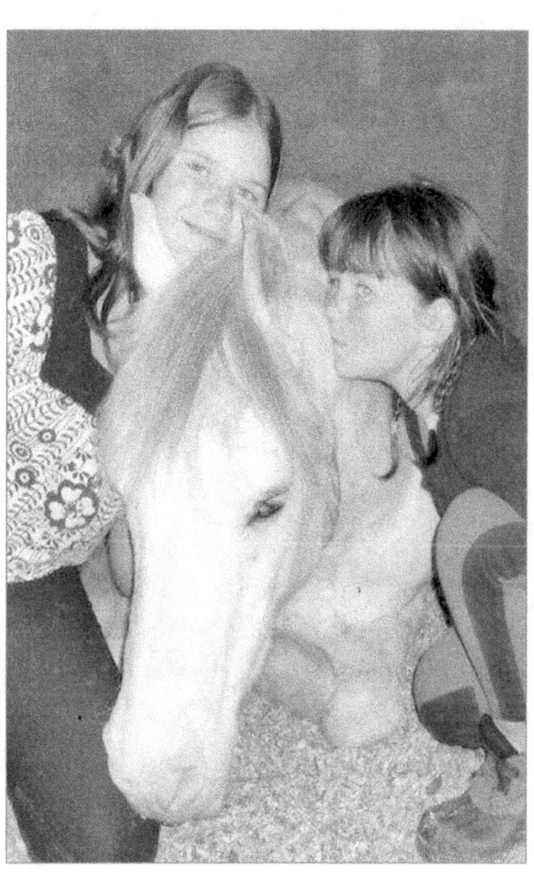

Some last thoughts

More grooming tips

When Spring arrives with its lighter evenings I spend more time with my horses and doing 'horsey' jobs. It is the time of year when they are losing their thick winter coats and hair gets everywhere.

• don't wear a woolly jumper when brushing horses as the hair sticks to it and you will spend more time brushing yourself

• waterproof overalls are ideal as hair falls straight off

• your horse will really appreciate a g o o d grooming to help bring out loose hair

• a gentle massage with the rubber curry comb will work wonders on his skin

• watch your horse as he stretches his neck and lifts his top lip. That's a sign you have found his itchy spot and he will love it!

Your tack should be checked regularly for wear and tear, for your horse's comfort and for your safety. Now is also a good time to give your grooming kit a thorough cleaning and marvel at where all those sweetie wrappers came from!

More cleaning tips

- wash all the brushes in warm soapy water

- wash the hoof oil brush last so it doesn't make the other brushes oily. Keep it in a plastic bag in your box

- replace perished sponges

- don't forget to clean the grooming kit box. A toothbrush is ideal as it can get into those awkward corners

It is also the time to check winter rugs before they are put away. You can do this on a large gate or stable door. Give it a thorough brushing on both sides with a dandy brush. Scrub it with warm, soapy water, rinse and leave it to dry. Use plaiting thread to sew any small tears.

Final last thoughts!

Horses are herd animals as you can see with these Przewalski horses below on Langeland in Denmark. Each horse will know his place in the

group. Some horses inherit leadership qualities. Most will grow up being followers. They have a strong survival instinct and you need to watch out for their habit of shying away or even bolting when unnerved in an Act Now, Think Later! manner.

Be aware of fireworks and loud noises such as motor cycles or cars passing too close or too fast. Horses are also wary of dogs and big vehicles if they are close by. Because horses are flight animals they will readily bolt if scared or spooked. Hopefully the training of car drivers with Wide and Slow posters when passing will keep you and your horse safe. Drivers also appreciate a smile or "thank you" when they observe this 'Horses on the Road' code!

Whatever their status, horses respond in a similar way to fear, excitement, anger and pleasure. Watch a group of them in a field all quietly munching or taking a nap when suddenly a plastic bag blows by. Their instinct tells them to shy away or up and flee from this 'horse-eating monster.' Only when they feel they are safe, or that perhaps it is only a plastic bag, will they stop and look. Inquisitive ones may take a closer look, while remaining cautious.

If a horse sees something new and refuses to pass it he will stand with his feet firmly on the ground on the edge of panic. To lead the horse calmly past, touch the object yourself if you are able, then stroke him. This should teach him how to conquer his fears. Shouting and punishment will make him associate strange objects with pain and discomfort.

Some horses are more insecure than others. If they don't respect the handler or rider as a leader, they won't trust him or her to keep them away from unsafe situations. They will also pick up on the rider's nervousness, especially from a beginner. This can make them more easily spooked about things, which can in turn make the rider more nervous.

A horse may fret if his companions are taken out of the field and he might gallop around calling for them until they return. Horses feel safer in large numbers, in a herd. They are, nevertheless, individual animals with likes and dislikes.

Treat all with patience and kindness and they will give their best back to you.

www.ingramcontent.com/pod-product-compliance
Lightning Source LLC
Chambersburg PA
CBHW080500030726
47592CB00011B/3194